Congressional Research Service

Bee Health: The Role of Pesticides

Linda-Jo Schierow
Specialist in Environmental Policy

Renée Johnson
Specialist in Agricultural Policy

M. Lynne Corn
Specialist in Natural Resources Policy

December 11, 2012

Congressional Research Service

7-5700

www.crs.gov

R42855

Summary

Bees, both commercially managed honey bees and wild bees, play an important role in global food production. In the United States, the value of honey bees only as commercial pollinators in U.S. food production is estimated at about $15 billion to $20 billion annually. The estimated value of other types of insect pollinators, including wild bees, to U.S. food production is not available. Given their importance to food production, many have expressed concern about whether a "pollinator crisis" has been occurring in recent decades. In the United States, commercial migratory beekeepers along the East Coast of the United States began reporting sharp declines in 2006 in their honey bee colonies. The U.S. Department of Agriculture (USDA) reports that overwinter colony losses from 2006 to 2011 averaged more than 32% annually. This issue remained legislatively active in the 110th Congress and resulted in increased funding for pollinator research, among other types of farm program support, as part of the 2008 farm bill (P.L. 110-246). Congressional interest in the health of honey bees and other pollinators has continued in the 112th Congress (e.g., H.R. 2381, H.R. 6083, and S. 3240) and may extend into the 113th Congress.

This report:

- Describes changes in managed and wild bee populations, given readily available data and information. It focuses on managed and wild bees only, and excludes other types of pollinators, including other insects, birds, and bats. Data on managed honey bees are limited, and do not provide a comprehensive view of changes in bee populations. Data for wild bee populations are even more limited.

- Provides a listing of the range of possible factors thought to be negatively affecting managed and wild bee populations. In addition to pesticides, other identified factors include bee pests and diseases, diet and nutrition, genetics, habitat loss and other environmental stressors, and beekeeping management issues, as well as the possibility that bees are being negatively affected by cumulative, multiple exposures and/or the interactive effects of each of these factors.

- Briefly summarizes readily available scientific research and analysis regarding the potential role of pesticides among the factors affecting the health and well-being of bees, as well as the statutory authority and related regulatory activities of the U.S. Environmental Protection Agency (EPA) related to pesticide use.

A 2007 report by the National Research Council of the National Academy of Sciences, *Status of Pollinators in North America,* provides a more detailed scientific context for this report and may be consulted for more in depth understanding about bee health. That study concluded that many factors contribute to pollinator declines in North America, and CRS accedes to that conclusion. Accordingly, the focus of this report on bee exposure to pesticides is not intended to imply that pesticides are any more important in influencing the health and wellness of bees than any of the other identified factors influencing bee health. Pesticides are only one of the many influences on bee health.

Because neonicotinoid pesticides have been the focus of concerns in Europe and in the United States, this report briefly describes recent scientific research related to possible effects of exposure to these pesticides on bees. The report concludes with a summary of recent regulatory activity regarding neonicotinoids at EPA, the federal agency charged with assessing risks and regulating U.S. sale and use of pesticides.

Contents

Figures

Tables

Contacts

B ees, both commercially managed honey bees and wild unmanaged bees, as well as many other types of insect pollinators, play an important role in global food production. In the United States, the value of honey bees only as commercial pollinators in U.S. food production is estimated at about $15 billion to $20 billion annually. The estimated value of other types of insect pollinators to U.S. food production is not available. Worldwide, the contribution of all insect pollinators—including commercial bees and wild bees—to the worldwide crop production used directly for human food is valued at €153 billion (or about $200 billion), according to the United Nations (UN).[1]

Given their importance to food production, many have expressed concern about whether a "pollinator crisis" has been occurring in recent decades. Worldwide reports indicate that populations of both managed honey bees and native bees have been declining, with colony losses in some cases described as severe or unusual. In Europe, managed honey bee colony numbers have been declining since the mid-1960s, and individual beekeepers have reported "unusual weakening and mortality in colonies," particularly during the period spanning winter through spring.[2] According to the United Nations, many insect pollinator species may be becoming rarer, causing some to question whether this is further sign of an overall global biodiversity decline.

In the United States, commercial migratory beekeepers along the East Coast of the United States began reporting sharp declines in their honey bee colonies starting in 2006. The U.S. Department of Agriculture (USDA) reports that overwinter colony losses from 2006 to 2011 averaged more than 32% annually. This issue was legislatively active in the 110th Congress and resulted in increased funding for pollinator research, among other types of farm program support, as part of the 2008 farm bill (P.L. 110-246).[3] Congressional interest in the health of honey bees and other pollinators has continued in the 112th (e.g., see H.R. 2381, H.R. 6083, and S. 3240) and may extend into the 113th Congress.

Reasons cited for U.S. bee population decreases include a wide range of possible factors thought to be negatively affecting pollinator species. For managed and wild bee populations, potential identified causes for these declines include bee pests and diseases, diet and nutrition, genetics, habitat loss and other environmental stressors, agricultural pesticides, and beekeeping management issues, as well as the possibility that bees are being negatively affected by cumulative, multiple exposures and/or the interactive effects of each of these factors. A 2007 report by the National Research Council of the National Academy of Sciences, *Status of Pollinators in North America*[4] (hereafter referred to as the "2007 NRC study") describes many of the factors affecting bee health and population effects.

Aside from the range of potential identified causes for bee colony declines, this report addresses what role, if any, pesticides play in influencing the health and wellness of bees. It begins by describing what is known about managed and wild bee populations, continues with brief descriptions of factors that might be affecting those populations, including a more detailed look at

---

[1] United Nations Environment Programme (UNEP), *Global Honey Bee Colony Disorders and Other Threats to Insect Pollinators*, UNEP Emerging Issues, 2010, http://www.unep.org/dewa/Portals/67/pdf/ Global_Bee_Colony_Disorder_and_Threats_insect_pollinators.pdf.

[2] Ibid.

[3] For more information, see CRS Report RL33938, *Honey Bee Colony Collapse Disorder*.

[4] National Academy of Sciences, National Research Council, 2007, *Status of Pollinators in North America*, http://www.nap.edu/catalog.php?record_id=11761. Hereafter referred to as the 2007 NRC study.

---

the potential effects of pesticide exposures, and concludes with a synopsis of pesticide risk management at the U.S. Environmental Protection Agency (EPA).

Background

More than 200,000 species of insects (bees, butterflies, moths, flies, wasps, beetles, ants), bats, birds and hummingbirds, and small mammals are plant pollinators. This report focuses on two categories of bees only:

- **Managed Honey Bees.** Honey bees (*Apis mellifera*; Family: Apidae) are the most well-known bee species. Honey bees are considered to be "social" bees in that they tend to work together in a highly structured social order, consisting of cooperation and division of labor within a colony, as well as the presence of two generations in a single nest at the same time. This same social behavior also allows for bees to be domesticated and managed. However, honey bees are only one of the world's estimated 17,000 described bee species, and one of the estimated total of 20,000 to 30,000 bee species worldwide.[5] Honey bees are not native to North America, but were introduced by European settlers in the 1600s.

- **Wild Bee Species.** An estimated 4,000 species of bees are native to North America.[6] With few exceptions, most of these are wild and not managed bees. Most types of wild bees are "solitary" bees—estimated at about 3,500 species—and do not have long-lived colonies.[7] Data and information on native bees are more limited than information on managed bees.

  The five most common families of native bees in North America are Andrenidae, Apidae, Colletidae, Halictidae, and Megachilidae. Andrenid bees are all ground nesters, and mostly comprise a large family of dark, non-descript bees, although some are colorful. Bees in the large Apidae family include not only honey bees, but also bumble bees (such as *Bombus* spp.), carpenter bees, squash or gourd bees, and others. Bees in the smaller Colletidae family are broader and wasp-like, and include plasterer bees. Bees in the Halictidae family include many species of sweat bees, and most have shiny metallic colored or black bodies. Bees in the Megachilidae family include resin and mason bees, orchard bees, and leaf-cutter bees that mostly nest in holes. Most families of bees contain some types of parasitic and cuckoo[8] bees. For a summary see text box below.

Both managed and wild bee species are critical to plant pollination and are economically valuable to U.S. agricultural production. In addition to honey bees, other types of bees are also managed, such as bumble bees, orchard bees, and alfalfa leaf-cutting bees. Some of these bees exhibit some of the social behaviors commonly associated with honey bees. These include bumble bees and some types of stingless bees.

---

[5] 2007 NRC study, p. 36; and S. Fecht, "Hive and Seek: Domestic Honeybees Keep Disappearing, but Are Their Wild Cousins in Trouble, Too?" *Scientific American*, May 8, 2012.

[6] Iowa State University, "Native Bees of North America," http://bugguide.net/node/view/475348.

[7] 2007 NRC study, p. 50; and Xerces Society, "Pollinator Conservation: Native Bee Biology," http://www.xerces.org/native-bees/.

[8] Refers to bees that lay their eggs in another bee's nest; as their eggs hatch early, the cuckoo larvae eat the other bee's provisions.

Only data on managed honey bees are readily available. Data and information on native bees are more limited. Where a few bee species are kept commercially and managed for their pollination services, wild bee species also play an important role in providing pollinator services to both commercial and small-scale home gardening systems.

Bee pollination of agricultural crops is said to contribute to the production of as many as 90 agricultural crops, including a wide range of high-value fruits, vegetables, tree nuts, forage crops, some field crops, and other specialty crops.[9] A number of agricultural crops are almost totally (90%-100%) dependent on animal pollination, including apples, avocados, blueberries, cranberries, cherries, kiwi fruit, macadamia nuts, asparagus, broccoli, carrots, cauliflower, celery, cucumbers, onions, legume seeds, pumpkins, squash, and sunflowers.[10] Other specialty crops also rely on pollination, but to a lesser degree. USDA reports that native bees also provide pollination services for a number of food crops. In addition to some of the aforementioned crops, these include alfalfa seeds, almonds, canola, chokecherries, grapefruit, pears, plums, prunes, soybeans (hybrid seed production), tomatoes, vegetable seeds, and watermelons.[11]

Classification of Bees

Kingdom   Animalia—Animal

    Phylum   Arthropoda—Arthropods

      Class   Insecta—insects, hexapoda

        Order   Hymenoptera—ants, bees, wasps

          Superfamily   Apoidea—bees, sphecoid wasps, apoid wasps

            Family   Andrenidae—andrenid bees, andrenids

            Family   Apidae—honey bees, bumble bees, carpenter bees, squash bees, stingless bees

            Family   Colletidae—colletid bees, plasterer bees, yellow-faced bees

            Family   Halictidae—halictid bees, sweat bees

            Family   Megachilidae—leafcutting bees, orchard bees, mason bees, resin bees

            Family   Melittidae—melittid bees, melittids

Source: Integrated Taxonomic Information System (ITIS), ITIS is supported by a consortium of federal and international agencies as well as scientific organizations to provide authoritative taxonomic information on known plant and animal species. Available at http://www.itis.gov/. Condensed and slightly modified by CRS to include more common names.

The economic value of pollination services provided by managed honey bees and wild bees is difficult to quantify. One widely cited estimate of the monetary value of honey bees as commercial pollinators in the United States is $14.6 billion annually.[12] Most of the estimated

---

[9] Staple crops (wheat, corn, and rice) do not rely on insect pollination and are mostly wind-pollinated.

[10] R. A. Morse and N. W. Calderone, *The Value of Honey Bees as Pollinators of U.S. Crops in 2000*, March 2000, Cornell University; and A.M. Klein, et. al., "Importance of pollinators in changing landscapes for world crops," *Proceedings of the Royal Society B: Biological Sciences*, Vol. 274, No. 1608, February 7, 2007.

[11] USDA, "Agroforestry: Sustaining Native Bee Habitat Crop Pollination," AF note-32, August 2006, http://plants.usda.gov/pollinators/Agroforestry_Sustaining_Native_Bee_Habitat_for_Crop_Pollination.pdf.

[12] R. A. Morse and N. W. Calderone, *The Value of Honey Bees as Pollinators of U.S. Crops in 2000*, March 2000, Cornell University, http://www.masterbeekeeper.org/pdf/pollination.pdf. This estimated value is measured according to (continued...)

value is attributable to alfalfa (mostly for alfalfa hay), apples, almonds, citrus, cotton, and soybeans. The 2007 NRC study reports other estimated values for honey bee pollination ranging from $5.7 billion—$19.0 billion annually.

For native bees, estimates of the economic value of pollination services are not readily available. However, a 2011 study by researchers at the University of California estimated that wild bee species add $0.9 billion to $2.4 billion per year in value to California's agriculture through pollination services.[13]

Changes in Bee Populations

Managed Honey Bees

There are an estimated 115,000-125,000 beekeepers in the United States.[14] Most of these (roughly 90,000-100,000) are hobbyists with fewer than 25 hives.[15] Commercial beekeepers tend to have more than 300 hives, and migrate their colonies during the year to provide pollination services to farmers. In the United States, most pollination services are provided by commercial beekeepers.[16]

USDA does not compile comprehensive annual survey data on honey bee colonies. Available data are limited and not ideal for evaluating population changes among honey bees. Annual data on the number of honey bee colonies are from statistics tracking the number of operations that produce honey for commercial sale. Additional data on all "colonies of bees" are from USDA's five-year *Census of Agriculture* (the most recent available data are for 2007 and 2002). These data are not strictly comparable: Data are compiled for different purposes—the latter tracks all farms with bee colonies, the former tracks operations that produce honey for commercial sale; also data are compiled using different data collection techniques—one is a periodic census, the other a statistical estimate. Generally, USDA data are mostly intended to track the number of honey-producing colonies; however, it is the value of managed bees as crop pollinators that provides perhaps the greatest economic impact in the production of food and feed crops.

Data from the most recent USDA *Census of Agriculture* indicate that 2.9 million bee colonies were on U.S. farms in 2007.[17] This compares to data from the previous *Census* in 2002 when

---

(...continued)

the additional value of production attributable to honey bees, in terms of the value of the increased yield and quality achieved from honey bee pollination, including the indirect benefits of bee pollination required for seed production of some crops.

[13] R. Chaplin-Kramer, et al., "Value of Wildland Habitat for Supplying Pollination Services to Californian Agriculture," Rangelands, June 2011, Vol. 33(3): 33-41.

[14] National Honey Bboard, "Beekeepers and Honeybee Colonies," http://www.honey.com/nhb/media/press-kit/. Data from 2012 industry survey, *Bee Culture* magazine.

[15] A colony of bees is composed of between 250—50,000 individual bees (Source: D. Sammataro and A. Avitabile, *The Beekeepers Handbook*, 4th Edition), although most larger, healthy, managed hives will have between 20,000—50,000 bees.

[16] These operations are able to supply a large number of honey bee colonies during the critical phase of a crop's bloom cycle, when bees pollinate a crop as they fly from flower to flower collecting nectar and pollen, which they carry back to the nest.

[17] USDA, *2007 Census of Agriculture*, Table 31, http://www.agcensus.usda.gov/Publications/2007/Full_Report/ Volume_1,_Chapter_1_US/st99_1_029_031.pdf.

---

there were about 2.4 million bee colonies, reflecting an increase in the total number of bee colonies. However, using similar data for the 1950s-1960s, there were an estimated 6 million managed honey bee colonies.[18] This may reflect ongoing consolidation and structural shifts in the U.S. agricultural sectors, rather than conclusive trends in species populations, abundance, and distribution.

USDA annual data for honey-producing colonies are similarly inconclusive. These data show year-to-year fluctuations, but not a clear downward trend over time (**Table 1**). Over the 10-year period shown, the number of bee colonies dropped from 2.6 million bee colonies in 2002 to 2.5 million bee colonies in 2011.[19] However, the endpoints mask a 10-year high in 2010 when honey production increased and the number of honey bee colonies reached nearly 2.7 million (**Table 1**). This increase in the number of honey-producing hives may reflect efforts among beekeepers to continually replenish their hives—either in response to a colony die-off or increase in the number of hives to raise overall honey production or to provide additional pollinator services. This increase might also reflect the rising popularity of beekeeping as a popular part-time hobby.

Table 1. Honey-Producing Bee Colonies, 2002-2011

Year	Colonies (1,000 colonies)	Honey Production (1,000 pounds)
2002	2,574	171,718
2003	2,599	181,727
2004	2,556	183,582
2005	2,413	174,818
2006	2,393	154,907
2007	2,443	148,341
2008	2,342	163,789
2009	2,498	146,416
2010	2,692	176,462
2011	2,491	148,357

Source: USDA, *Honey,* http://usda.mannlib.cornell.edu/MannUsda/viewDocumentInfo.do?documentID=1191. Honey producing colonies for producers with 5 or more colonies. Areas with the most honey bee colonies include North and South Dakota; California; Florida; Montana, Minnesota, Idaho, and Texas. Other major states are Michigan, Oregon, Georgia, Nebraska, New York, Washington, Wisconsin, and Wyoming.

Among all honey bee colonies, more than 2 million are reported to belong to commercial migratory beekeepers and are rented each year to pollinate U.S. agricultural crops. An estimated 1.5 million colonies are needed each year to pollinate California's 750,000 acres of almond trees alone.[20] Increasingly bee colony rentals are being used to pollinate cultivated blueberries in the East Coast states and in the Midwest.[21] Other information indicates that bee colonies are also

---

[18] Presentation to Congressional staff by Jeff Pettis, USDA/Agricultural Research Service, June 18, 2012.

[19] USDA, *Honey,* March 2012 http://usda.mannlib.cornell.edu/MannUsda/viewDocumentInfo.do?documentID=1191.

[20] C. Souza, "What's the buzz about pollination?" *California Country* magazine, March/April 2011.

[21] See, for example, "Honey Bees and Blueberry Pollination," Fact Sheet 629, University of Maine Extension, April 2002.

rented for apple, pear, plum, cherry, cranberry, avocado, cucumber, kiwi fruit, melon, pepper, and citrus fruit production, as well as for alfalfa, clover seed, and sunflower production.[22] Both locally and globally, some are concerned that the availability of honey bee stocks is not keeping pace with growing agricultural demands for pollination services.[23]

The 2007 NRC study voices concerns about the available USDA data on honey bees, cautioning against use of these data to determine changes in honey bee populations. Concerns about these data, including: the purpose of these data is to track U.S. honey production not bee populations; lack of comparability among the available data compilations; the potential for misidentification of species and miscounting because of data collection procedures; and other issues.[24]

Notwithstanding these concerns about data availability and quality, the 2007 NRC study concluded: "Long-term population trends for the honey bee, the most important managed pollinator, are demonstrably downward."[25] Honey bee colony losses are not uncommon. The 2007 NRC study cites USDA data showing honey bee declines in 1947–1972, and 1989–1996, as well as declines starting in 2005 (despite reports of a sharp rise in 2010). These downward trends have continued since that study was published, attributable to what is now known as Colony Collapse Disorder (CCD), which is thought to have affected mostly managed bee colonies starting in late 2006.

As reported by USDA: "The defining characteristic of CCD is the disappearance of most, if not all, of the adult honey bees in a colony, leaving behind honey and brood (immature bees confined to cells in the hive, including larvae and pupae) but no dead bee bodies."[26] Scientists at USDA and bee labs across the country have been looking for the cause or causes of CCD within four broad categories:[27]

- Pathogens (such as *Nosema ceranae*);

- Parasites (such as *Varroa* mites);

- Environmental stressors (such as pesticides or lack of nectar diversity); and also

- Management stressors (such as transportation stress by migratory beekeepers).

---

[22] Penn State University, "A Year in the Life of a Migratory Honey Bee Colony;" M. Burgett, *1999 Pacific Northwest Honey Bee Pollination Survey*, Oregon State University; and Brenda Kiessling, presentation at Green Spring Garden Park's "EcoSavvy Symposium," Virginia, February 2012.

[23] See, for example, M. A. Aizen and L. D. Harder, "The Global Stock of Domesticated Honey Bees is growing Slower than Agricultural Demand for Pollination," *Current Biology*, May 2009.

[24] 2007 NRC study, p. 3.

[25] Ibid.

[26] J. Kim Kaplan, "Colony Collapse Disorder: An Incomplete Puzzle," *Agricultural Research* (USDA publication), July 2012, http://www.ars.usda.gov/is/AR/archive/jul12/colony0712.htm. For other information, see CRS Report RL33938, *Honey Bee Colony Collapse Disorder*. The definition of CCD was recently revised to include other probably contributing factors, such as low levels of *Varroa* mite and other pathogens, such as *Nosema*, which appear to be associated with most winter colony losses. (Also see Benjamin Dinat, Jay D. Evans, Yan Ping Chen, et al., 2012, "Predictive markers of honey bee colony collapse," *PLoS ONE*, vol. 7, no. 2 (p. e32151).

[27] J. Kim Kaplan, op. cit.

As reported by USDA in July 2012: "While many possible causes for CCD have been proposed, reported, and discussed—both in the scientific literature and popular media—no cause has been proven."[28] These and other factors are discussed in "Identified Factors Affecting Bee Health".

Heightened attention following concerns about CCD has resulted in better tracking by USDA of annual honey bee colony losses. USDA reports that before 2006 bee colony losses averaged 15%-20% per year since the 1990s, attributable to a variety of factors, such as mites, diseases, and management stress. By comparison, bee colony losses between the winters of 2006/2007 and 2010/2011 averaged more than 32% during the year: Surveys found total colony losses of:[29]

- 30% in the winter of 2010/2011;

- 34% in the winter of 2009/2010;

- 29% in the winter of 2008/2009;

- 36% in the winter of 2007/2008;

- 32% in the winter of 2006/2007.

Other information from USDA indicates that colony losses range from 7% to 80% loss, depending on area.[30] Preliminary survey results indicate that total losses of managed honey bee colonies from all causes were 22% nationwide for the 2011/2012 winter, representing a substantial improvement in mortality compared to the previous five years.[31]

The leading causes of declining bee populations cited in the 2007 NRC study—which was published before CCD became a well-publicized phenomenon—included pathogens and introduced parasites, particularly *Varroa destructor*, the varroa mite. That study, among others, documents the extensive, but still inconclusive literature on honey bee population losses due to bee pests, parasites, pathogens, and disease, as well as other causes.

Native Bees

While managed bees are commercially important, wild bee species are important ecologically for sustainable forests and fields. No comprehensive formal statistics are available on populations of wild bees in the United States, despite numerous attempts to promote the use of various informal "citizen science" initiatives in California, Florida, other East Coast states, and elsewhere.[32] As

---

[28] Ibid.

[29] Dennis vanEngelsdorp, Jay Hayes, and Jeff Pettis, 2009, "Preliminary Results: A Survey of Honey Bee Colonies Losses in the U.S. between September 2008 and April 2009." Survey based on about 20% of all U.S. colonies.

[30] Jeff Pettis, "Colony Collapse Disorder Affecting Honey Bee (*Apis mellifera*) Colonies," October 2008 presentation, http://www.epa.gov/pesticides/ppdc/2008/oct2008/session7-ccd.pdf. Survey based on 22 operations, managing 10% of U.S. colonies, and AIA surveys.

[31] D. vanEngelsdorp, J. Pettis, K. Rennich, et al., 2012, "Preliminary Results: Honey Bee Colony Losses in the U.S., Winter 2011-2012," http://beeinformed.org/2012/05/winter2012/; K. Rennich, J. Pettis, D. vanEngelsdorp, et al., 2012, "2011-2012 National Honey Bee Pests and Diseases Survey Report," http://www.aphis.usda.gov/plant_health/plant_pest_info/honey_bees/downloads/2011_National_Survey_Report.pdf; and USDA, "Survey by USDA and Collaborators Reports Fewer Winter Honey Bee Losses," May 31, 2012, http://www.ars.usda.gov/is/pr/2012/120531.htm.

[32] See, for example, the University of California's backyard bee count (http://www.greatsunflower.org/), the University of Florida's "Native Buzz" project (http://www.ufnativebuzz.com/), and the "Bee Hunt" project organized by multiple (continued...)

---

already noted, an estimated 3,500 species are solitary bees, and these species are not readily surveyed. Roughly an additional 500 species of bees native to North America show some degree of social behavior. Scientific literature is replete with assertions about the paucity of data on one group or another of native bees. Long term data are particularly difficult to obtain for wild bees. As concluded by the researchers in the 2007 NRC study, among all wild pollinators:

> There is evidence of decline in the abundance of some pollinators, but the strength of this evidence varies among taxa. Long-term population trends for several wild bee species (notably bumble bees) ... are notably downward. For most pollinator species, however, the paucity of long-term population data and the incomplete knowledge of even basic taxonomy and ecology make definitive assessment of status exceedingly difficult. [33]

In the absence of comprehensive data, the following section describes selected information gained about particular taxa or sites since the publication of the 2007 NRC study. As some of the studies cited below demonstrate, scientists seeking to find any data to analyze broad pollinator trends might be forced to rely on amalgamations of disparate studies, collections by citizen scientists,[34] and other unconventional approaches.

Timing of Bees and Associated Flowering Plants

A 2011 paper showed that the phenological changes in flowering times were accompanied by changes in the spring emergence of bee populations.[35] Reviewing a number of previous studies on flowering times and pollination, the investigators found that ten species of bees (including both solitary and social species) had advanced to earlier dates in the spring for their first emergence, and the flowering times of the plants they visited also advanced. Advances in emergence time over the period from 1970-2010 were highly significant. Various hypotheses to explain the difference were examined; the data "[support] the idea that climate change is the main factor explaining the observed phenological advances." However, the authors "conclude that phenological mismatch probably has not occurred already, but that it could occur in the future, as rates of temperature warming increase." At the same time, the study noted that it analyzed generalist bees and generalist flowers—bees that visit many plant species, and plants visited by many bee species.[36] Where the life cycles of particular bee species are tied to particular plant species, different trends may occur. While no data were reported on the population sizes of these bees, in this study there was no clear connection between climate change (as measured by

---

(...continued)

university staff, federal agencies, and private partnerships (http://www.discoverlife.org/bee/index.html).

[33] 2007 NRC study, p. 7. See also 2007 NRC study, p. 88 (referring to *Bombus*, or bumble bees) ; p. 29 (referring to pollinators generally in North America); and p. 203 (referring to the absence of baseline data on pollinator status generally as an impediment to estimation of any decline).

[34] A well-known example of citizen-scientist-based data in North America is the annual Christmas bird count, which has been conducted for nearly a century in some areas. Data may not serve for some quantitative analyses, but may be much more reliable for the presence or absence of a bird, for example. In other studies, on arrival dates at bird feeders, or bees on spring flowers, the date on which a species is first observed could be another relatively reliable observation.

[35] I. Bartomeus, J.S. Ascher, D. Wagner, et al., 2011, "Climate-associated phenological advances in bee pollinators and bee-pollinated plants," *Proceedings of the National Academy of Sciences*, v. 108, n. 51, pp. 20645-20649. *Phenology* is the scientific study of biological phenomena that are cyclical or periodic. Examples include migration, hibernation, and nesting, as well as flowering times. Phenology is particularly important in analysis of climate change.

[36] The species studied were in four genera: *Andrena* (three species), *Bombus* (two species), *Colletes* (one species), and *Osmia* (four species).

---

flowering times) and any harm to the species studied. The bees seemed to be keeping up with the changes in dates of flower availability.

In 2010, an international group of scientists reviewed global trends in pollinator species, including bees.[37] They cited a study based on data gathered by citizen-scientists in the United Kingdom and in the Netherlands (number of years of observation varying by location) showing that "in both countries, bee diversity has fallen significantly in most landscapes.... Analysis of pollinator traits demonstrated that in bees ..., specialist (diet and/or habitat) and sedentary species tended to decline, whereas mobile generalists tended to thrive." As the authors also noted:[38]

> The parallel dynamics between plants and their pollinators suggest a link between the two, although this is correlative and the mechanism is as yet unknown. It could be that plant declines are caused, in part, by a lack of pollination services, or bees could be declining owing to a lack of floral resources, or indeed both could be declining owing to shared sensitivity to environmental changes.

Bumble Bees

Compared to most native species, bumble bees (*Bombus*) are better studied. According to the 2007 NRC report, there are 239 species of bumble bees worldwide; of these, 60 species are found in the U.S., Mexico, and Canada.[39] Some species are managed in controlled environments to pollinate greenhouse tomatoes. Others are valued as primary or supplementary pollinators for members of the squash family such as cucumbers, watermelons, and cantaloupes.

In the United States, citizens are recruited to gather data on these large insects—for example, forming Bumble Bee Brigades in one campaign.[40] Even so, information about the wild bumble bees is not comprehensive. One species (*B. franklini*) is thought to be extinct in its very limited (former) range in northeastern California and southeastern Oregon. Hoping to establish trends for some species, some scientists examined both museum collection records and intensive nationwide surveys for records of abundance and distribution of eight species of this genus.[41] Four species have declined in relative abundance by up to 96%. These four also contracted their ranges by 23% to 87%. These changes were statistically highly significant; the other four species showed no clear pattern in terms of range reduction. The authors hypothesized that the four declining species may be affected by a pathogen (*Nosemi bombi*) as well as reduced genetic diversity.[42] The data were adequate only to show an association, rather than a cause—were the four species declining because of the disease and low genetic diversity? Or was some other factor causing these species

---

[37] S.G. Potts, J.C. Biesmeijer, C. Kremen, et al., 2010, "Global pollinator declines: trends, impacts and drivers," *Trends in Ecology and Evolution*, v. 25, n. 6, pp. 345-353.

[38] Ibid.

[39] 2007 NRC report, p. 43.

[40] The University of Wyoming, through its Berry Center, sponsors the program. See http://www.uwyo.edu/berrycenter/citizen-science/bumblebees.html for more information.

[41] S.A. Cameron, J.D. Lozier, and J.P. Strange, et al., 2011, "Patterns of widespread decline in North American bumble bees," *Proceedings of the National Academy of Sciences*, v. 108, n. 2, pp. 662-667.

[42] The authors also noted that some believe that *Nosema bombi* was introduced via commercially imported European bumble bees, and North American bumble bees may therefore have less resistance to the disease than European species. They compare the impacts of the pathogen to the fungal infections currently devastating wild populations of amphibians and bats.

to decline and making them more susceptible to the disease and also reducing their genetic diversity?

Stingless Bees

Meliponine bees, with about 400 species, belong to the same family (Apidae) as bumble bees and honey bees.[43] Commonly called *stingless bees*, they are found in the tropics, and were widely cultivated by Native Americans in Central and South America before the introduction of honey bees from Europe. While they do not sting, most species can inflict a serious bite. A few species can produce a secretion from their mouth parts; added to a bite, the secretion may produce blisters. Loss of forest cover eliminates nesting sites. The shift by beekeepers to honey bees for more intensive production has also reduced the number of stingless bees. An analysis of the effects of forestry on stingless bees in Brazil observed that most bee nests were found in hollow trees over 50 cm (~20 inches) in diameter.[44] Given the high value of the bees as pollinators for many species of plants, and the low commercial value of hollow trees, the authors recommended that managed forests maintain hollow trees as both seed sources and as homes for these bees.[45] In addition, some studies suggest that stingless bees are especially susceptible to some pesticides.[46]

Interactions of Bees and Associated Flowers: Trophic Cascade

The phenomenon known as *trophic cascade* may also play a role in the interaction of pollinator species. Many plants can be pollinated by more than one species, and many bee species use more than one pollen or nectar source. As individual pollinator species (bees or other species) decline, other species may take over the declining species' role. Where the data are available (as with the *Bombus* study cited above), evidence suggests that, where a generalist bee species is able to step in to provide pollination services (even if less able than a specialist bee), the effects of a reduced bee population may be masked by the generalist. In more concrete terms, the presence of a highly efficient generalist—like the honey bee—may mask the loss of native species (regardless of the reason for the decline of the native species). If honey bees themselves then decline, the effects of the lost population may be more severe because populations of back-up pollinators have already been reduced or eliminated. And conversely, reductions in honey bee populations may reduce competition sufficiently to allow other (reduced) bee populations to rebound to greater numbers.

Identified Factors Affecting Bee Health

Factors that have been identified to be negatively affecting managed and native bee populations are (listed in no particular order):[47]

---

[43] 2007 NRC report, p. 48.

[44] G. C. Venturieri, 2009, "The impact of forest exploitation on Amazonian stingless bees (Apidae Meliponini)," *Genetics and Molecular Research*, v. 8, n. 2, pp. 684-689.

[45] Ibid.

[46] H.V.V. Tomé, G.F. Martins, et al., 2012, "Imidacloprid-induced impairment of mushroom bodies and behavior of the native stingless bee Melipona quadrifasciata anthidioides," *PLoS ONE*, v. 7, n. 6, p. e38406, http://www.plosone.org/article/info%3Adoi%2F10.1371%2Fjournal.pone.0038406.

[47] Compiled by CRS from multiple sources (2007 NRC study; USDA, *Colony Collapse Disorder Progress Report*, CCD Steering Committee, June 2011; comments by Laurie Adams, North American Pollinator Protection Campaign (continued...)

- **parasites, pathogens, and diseases** (for a detailed listing, see text box);

- **bee genetics** including lack of genetic diversity and lineage of bees, and increased susceptibility and lowered disease resistance, and also miticide resistance by the mites;[48]

- **diet and nutrition** including poor nutrition due to apiary overcrowding, pollination of crops with low nutritional value, and pollen or nectar scarcity associated with invasive plants;

- **bee management issues** including transportation stress from migratory beekeeping, overcrowding, feeding practices, chemicals used by beekeepers to control mites (antibiotics and miticides), confinement and temperature fluctuations, susceptibility to disease, potential for cumulative exposure to diseases and parasites, use of bees for honey production versus pollination, chemical residue or contamination in the wax, and reliability of the queen source;

- **habitat loss, and other environmental or biological stressors** including loss of foraging area, interspecific competition between native and non-native bees, pathogen spillover effects, and climate change;

- **pesticides** including acute or cumulative exposure to new types and combinations of agricultural pesticides through a variety of media including dust, water droplets, pollen, and nectar;

- **other agricultural practices** including the use of genetically incorporated pesticides in seeds or treated seeds, such as with bioengineered crops; and

- **potential cumulative and interactive effects** of each of these factors.

These same factors were among those initially thought to be contributing to CCD. As outlined in USDA's 2011 progress report, the available research over the past few years on the numerous possible causes for CCD has led USDA and university researchers to conclude that "no single factor or specific combination of factors has been identified as a 'cause' [for CCD]."[49] This has led researchers to further examine the hypothesis that CCD may be "a syndrome caused by many different factors, working in combination or synergistically;"[50] it may also involve "an interaction between pathogens and other stress factors."[51] USDA reports that researchers are continuing to focus in three major areas: (1) pesticides that may be having unexpected negative effects on honey bees; (2) a parasite or pathogen that may be attacking honey bees, including the pathogenic gut fungus, *Nosema*, as well as viral infections; and (3) a combination of existing stresses that may compromise the immune system of bees and disrupt their social system, making colonies more susceptible to disease and collapse.[52]

(...continued)

(NAPPC) in a presentation to Congressional staff on June 18, 2012.

[48] A miticide is a pesticide intended to kill mites.

[49] USDA, *CCD Progress Report*, June 2011, http://www.ars.usda.gov/is/br/ccd/ccdprogressreport2011.pdf.

[50] USDA, *CCD Progress Report*, June 2009, http://www.ars.usda.gov/is/br/ccd/ccdprogressreport.pdf.

[51] D. vanEngelsdorp, J.D. Evans, C. Saegerman, et al., 2009, "Colony collapse disorder: A descriptive study," *PLOS One*, v. 4, n. 8, (August), e6481. doi:10.1371/journal.pone.0006481, http://www.plosone.org/article/info:doi/10.1371/journal.pone.0006481.

[52] USDA, "Q&A: Colony Collapse Disorder," http://www.ars.usda.gov/News/docs.htm?docid=15572.

Pests and Diseases Affecting Honey Bees

As noted in the 2007 NRC study, among the leading causes of managed honey bee losses are diseases, parasites, and recently introduced competitors. Most notable are declines due to two parasitic mites, the so-called vampire mite (*Varroa destructor*) and the tracheal mite (*Acarapis woodi*). Also of concern is the emergence of new or newly virulent fungal and viral diseases. New invasive pests are also harming bees.

Below is a brief listing of some identified pests and diseases. For more information, see the 2007 NRC report and other beekeeper guidance documents. The following is mainly excerpted from *The Beekeepers Handbook*.

Honey bee diseases may be caused by a protozoan (e.g., bacteria or amoeba), fungus, or virus.

- **Nosema disease** is the most common adult bee disease, and is caused by a microscopic fungus (formerly considered to be a protozoan). Two *Nosema* species are found in honey bees: (1) *Nosema apis*; and (2) *Nosema ceranae* (the more virulent of the two).

- **American Foulbrood Disease (AFD)** is the most destructive of brood diseases. (Brood refers to the egg, larval, and pupal stages in bee development.) AFD is caused by a bacterium (*Paenibacillus larvae*) that exists in a spore or a vegetative stage; the disease is transmitted by the spore and the infected brood is killed by the vegetative stage.

- **European Foulbrood Disease (EFD)** is also caused by a bacterium (*Melissococcus plutonius*) and is commonly found in colonies already weakened by lack of food or by other stressors.

- **Chalkbrood disease** is caused by a fungus (*Ascophaera apis*); adult bees can detect and remove diseased larvae; honey production may be reduced but the disease usually will not destroy a colony.

- **Amoeba disease** is caused by the amoeba *Malpighamoeba mellificae* Prell; it infests the gut of honey bees. Resistant spores (cysts) form in honey bees and can transmit the disease to other bees.

- Other less common adult diseases include **septicemia** and **spiroplasma**. Both are caused by bacteria. The former cause destruction of connective tissues; the latter infects the bees' blood. They tend to cause dysentery, and arise primarily from poor food and long periods of confinement.

- Some common **viral diseases** affecting honey bees include: Deformed Wing Virus (DWV); Black Queen Cell Virus (BQCV); Israeli Acute Paralysis Virus (IAPV); Acute Bee Paralysis Virus (ABPV); Sacbrood Virus (SBV); Kashmir Bee Virus; and Chronic Bee Paralysis Virus (CBPV).

Other pests are mostly invertebrates, but some vertebrates are problematic locally. Among these pests are parasitic mites, insects, and some larger animals.

- **Tracheal mites** (*Acarapis woodi*) are parasitic mites that live inside the breathing organs of adult bees, and eventually a newly mated female mite emerges from the old host bee.

- **Varroa mites**, now known mostly for the vampire mite (*Varroa destructor*), are large mites that feed on infested bees, resulting in disfigured, stunted adult bees and deformed larvae and pupae (varroosis).

- Emerging threats such as the parasitic **phorid fly** (*Apocephalus borealis*), known to parasitize bumble bees, has been found to also parasitize honey bees and can eventually cause bees to abandon their hives.

- **Major insect enemies** include the wax moth, and the small hive beetle.

- **Minor insect enemies** include assassin and ambush bugs, robber flies, mantids, wasps, and dragonflies.

- Various **vertebrate pests** include skunks, raccoons, bears, and mice.

One **competitor** deserves mention—the introduced Africanized honey bee. This bee is also a honey bee (*Apis mellifera*) but of a different strain from those imported from Europe. They are good foragers, but the colonies are more difficult to manage than the domestic European bee; they are sometimes called "killer bees" although an individual bee's sting is no more severe than that of a European bee. They were accidentally released in Brazil decades ago and have spread into the southern United States.

Sources: D. Sammataro and A. Avitabile, The Beekeepers Handbook, 4th Edition, pp. 189-232; Beekeepers Association of Northern Virginia, "Diseases, Parasites, Pests, and Predators," presentation materials; and for phorid flies, see A. Core, et al., "A New Threat to Honey Bees, the Parasitic Phorid Fly *Apocephalus borealis*," PLoS ONE 7(1), January 3, 2012, http://www.plosone.org/article/info:doi%2F10.1371%2Fjournal.pone.0029639.

Possible Role of Pesticides

The previous section lists a range of possible factors thought to be negatively affecting managed and wild bee populations. Among the identified factors were bee pests and diseases, diet and nutrition, genetics, habitat loss and other environmental stressors, beekeeper issues, and pesticides, as well as possible negative effects of cumulative, multiple exposures and/or the interactive effects of each of these factors.

In response to congressional requests, this section examines in greater detail the potential role of pesticides, providing a summary of selected, readily available data and reviews of the scientific literature. This focus on the potential role of pesticides is not intended to imply that pesticides are as important or more important in influencing the health and wellness of bee colonies as compared with other identified factors influencing bee health; the relative importance of pesticides in U.S. or global bee health is unknown and a subject of numerous research projects, some of which are discussed below. In addition, this section summarizes general information about the nature of pesticides, pesticide uses, and pesticide regulation in the United States, as well as more specific information about the registration status of a class of pesticides known as neonicotinoids.

Pesticides and Pesticide Law

Pesticides are broadly defined in U.S. law as chemicals and other products used to kill, repel, or control pests.[53] Familiar examples include pesticides used to kill insects (insecticides) and weeds (herbicides) that can reduce the yield, and sometimes harm the quality, of agricultural crops, ornamental plants, forests, wooden structures (e.g., through termite damage), and pastures. But the broad legal definition of "pesticide" also applies to products with less familiar "pesticidal uses." For example, substances are pesticides when used to control mites, mold, mildew, and other nuisance growths in hives or on equipment. The term also applies to disinfectants and sterilizing agents, animal repellents, rat poison, and many other substances. An estimated 18,000 pesticide products are currently in use in the United States.[54] Pesticides vary greatly in toxicity, persistence in the environment, and ability to bioaccumulate up the food chain, as well as in the range of plants and animals that are likely to be affected in the event of exposure. Some are practically nontoxic to some species but exquisitely toxic to other species.

Statutory Framework

All pesticides are regulated by EPA under the authority of the Federal Insecticide, Fungicide, and Rodenticide Act (FIFRA), but approximately 5,800 pesticide products used in food production also are regulated under the Federal Food, Drug, and Cosmetic Act (FFDCA), Section 408. FIFRA requires EPA to regulate the sale and use of pesticides in the United States through product registration and labeling. EPA is required to regulate so as to prevent unreasonable adverse effects on people and the environment, taking into account the costs and benefits of various pesticide uses. FIFRA prohibits sale of any pesticide in the United States unless it is

---

[53] Federal Insecticide, Fungicide, and Rodenticide Act, Section 2(u). 7 U.S.C. 136-136y. For more detailed information about pesticide laws and regulations, see CRS Report RL31921, *Pesticide Law: A Summary of the Statutes.*

[54] S. Kaiser, EPA, personal communication with CRS staff, December 16, 2011.

registered (licensed) and labeled to indicate approved uses and restrictions. It is a violation of the law to use a pesticide in a manner that is inconsistent with the label instructions. EPA registers each pesticide product for each approved use. For example, a product may be registered for use on bee hives to control mites or as a seed treatment for corn. In addition, FIFRA requires EPA to reregister pesticides first registered prior to 1984 and to review all registered pesticides periodically on a 15-year cycle based on new data that meet current regulatory and scientific standards.

For the 600 or more pesticides (i.e., active ingredients) registered for use in food production, section 408 of the FFDCA authorizes EPA to establish maximum allowable residue levels (also known as "tolerances") to ensure that human exposure to the pesticide ingredients in food and animal feed will be "safe."[55] A "safe" tolerance is defined in the law as a level at which there is "a reasonable certainty of no harm" from the exposure, even when considering total cumulative and aggregate pesticide exposure of children. (This standard also is used in registering pesticides for residential uses.) Under the FFDCA, foods (or animal feeds) with a residue of a pesticide ingredient for which there is no tolerance established, or with a residue level exceeding an established tolerance limit, are declared "unsafe" and "adulterated"; such foods cannot be sold in interstate commerce or imported to the United States. Pesticides may not be registered under FIFRA for use on food crops unless tolerances (or exemptions) have been established under the FFDCA.

Registration Process

When pesticide manufacturers apply to register an "active" ingredient for a pesticide, a commercial pesticide product, or a new use of a registered pesticide under FIFRA Section 3, EPA requires them to submit scientific data on toxicity and behavior in the environment. EPA may require data from any combination of more than 100 different tests, depending on the potential toxicity of active and inert ingredients and degree of exposure. To register a pesticide for use on food, EPA also requires applicants to determine the amount of residue that could remain on crops, as well as on (or in) food products (such as corn syrup), assuming that the pesticide product is applied according to the manufacturers' recommended rates and methods. Based on the data submitted, EPA determines whether and under what conditions a proposed pesticide use would present an unreasonable risk to human health or the environment, and, for a food or residential use, whether its use would be safe. Some features of pesticides that might affect registration decisions include the specificity of the pesticide for the targeted pest, its toxicity to people who apply it, its tendency to persist in the environment over time, and its ability to bioaccumulate in animals higher in the food chain. EPA specifically takes into account unintended harm to bees and available information for other nontargeted insects in its registration decisions. EPA requires studies to determine acute (short-term) toxicity of a pesticide on individual bees when they come into body contact with pesticide residue. EPA also collects reports on bee-kill incidents. If a pesticide appears to be very toxic to bees, EPA may require long-term studies of its effects.

---

[55] Ingredients in pesticide products are categorized as active or inert. Active ingredients are those that are intended to control the pest, while inert ingredients, now generally known as "other ingredients," are used to deliver the active ingredients effectively to the pest. Other ingredients often are solvents or surfactants and often comprise the bulk of the pesticide product. Some inerts are known to be toxic, some are known to be harmless, and others have unknown toxicity.

If the risk is determined to be unreasonable or unsafe, EPA attempts to mitigate the risk by adjusting requirements on the label (for example, requiring a buffer zone around lakes and streams or requiring personal protective equipment for pesticide handlers). If the risk remains unreasonable or unsafe, EPA will refuse to register the pesticide. If the risk is determined to be reasonable and safe, registration is granted and the agency specifies the approved uses and conditions of use, including safe methods of pesticide storage and disposal, which the registrant must explain on the product label. EPA can and often does require specific application methods to be printed on the product label to minimize environmental damage. For example, the label sometimes requires that application of certain pesticides occur when bees are not foraging, when there is little wind, or in a granular form or as a seed coating rather than aerially, in order to minimize spray drift off property. Pesticide registrations are reviewed at least once every 15 years to consider new scientific information and may be reviewed at any time in response to reports of adverse effects and possible unreasonable risks from use of particular pesticides.

Exposure to Pesticides

Beekeepers use pesticides registered for the control of bacteria, fungi, mites, and other bee pests. These are meant to protect bees from diseases. These pesticides are applied within and in the vicinity of hives. Some common pesticides applied deliberately to hives include formic acid, thymol, coumaphos, and fluvalinate.

Bees also sometimes are exposed to pesticides accidentally, either when pesticides are misused or misapplied, or when used according to label directions to control pests in areas frequented by bees, for example, alongside roads or rights of way for the control of weeds, trees, or other pests; on or near commercial farm crops; or on or near fields, lawns, and gardens to control fleas, ticks, weeds, grubs, mosquitos, or other adult insects. **Figure 1** illustrates some significant paths of exposure to pesticides applied as a spray or as a soil or seed treatment (systemic) for bees. If bees happen to fly through a newly treated field or dust clouds from planting of seeds coated with pesticide, or if they are orally exposed to pesticide in food or water, and if exposure is high enough, bees may be sickened or die from pesticide exposure. (See summaries of specific studies below.)

Impacts of Pesticides on Bee Health

As explained above, little is known about the health over time of native bees in the United States. The health of managed honey bees is better characterized, but still somewhat uncertain. Therefore, it is not appropriate at this time to conclude there has been a general and significant decline in native bees, or to attribute global or even North American declines in the health of any particular species of bee either native or managed bee species to pesticides. On the other hand, pesticides are known to have some adverse local impacts on honey bees and some native bees. Widespread use of herbicides reduces habitat available to bees;[56] many pesticides are known to be acutely toxic to bees, given sufficient levels of exposure; and some reports of local bee kill incidents have been well documented. Laboratory research has shown lethal and sub-lethal effects on individual bees associated with exposure to numerous pesticides. According to research cited

---

[56] J.H. Cane and V.J. Tepedino, 2001, "Causes and extent of declines among native North American invertebrate pollinators: Detection, evidence, and consequences," *Conservation Ecology*, v. 5, n. 1, p. 1, http://www.ecologyandsociety.org/vol5/iss1/art1/.

by the NRC, "The application of pesticides, especially insecticides used to control crop pests, kills or weakens thousands of honey bee colonies in the United States each year."[57] Nevertheless, the NRC concluded in its 2007 report that *local* bee kills "likely have not contributed significantly to the recent *national* decline in colony populations" [emphasis added].[58]

Figure 1. Major Routes of Exposure of Foraging Bees to Pesticides

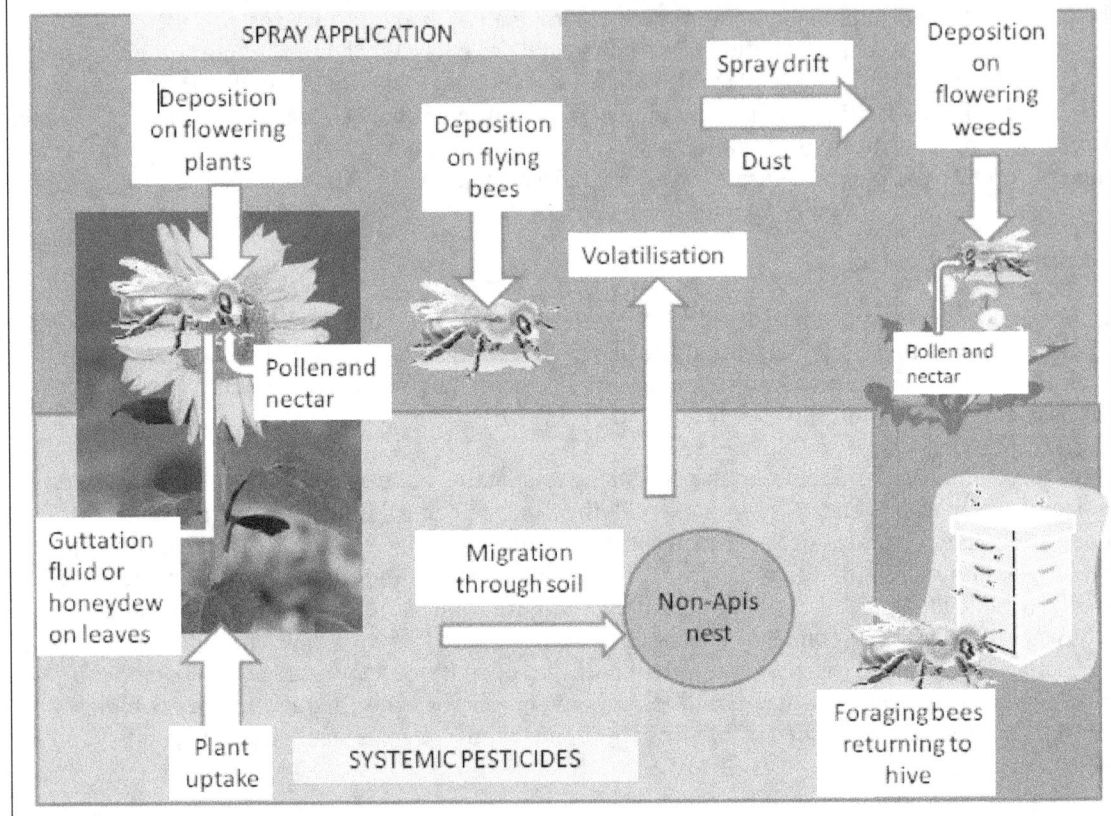

Source: European Food Safety Authority (EFSA), "Scientific Opinion on the science behind the development of a risk assessment of Plant Protection Products on bees (*Apis mellifera, Bombus* spp. and solitary bees)," Figure 3.1, EFSA-Q-2011-00417, May 2012, http://www.efsa.europa.eu/en/efsajournal/pub/2668.htm.

Five years after the NRC issued its report, generalizations about the relative importance of pesticides for global bee health still cannot be drawn from available data, given the disparate study designs and results. Moreover, although research has been and continues to be conducted, most scientists have focused on a single pesticide or pathogen at a time and consideration of interactions has been minimal. A 2010 article by a group of well-known researchers explains:

> Attempts to correlate global bee declines or CCD with increased pesticide exposures alone, have not been successful to date ... Pesticide interactions among various mixtures as well as with other stressors including *Varroa* and *Nosema*, IAPV, beneficial hive microbes, and impacts on bee

---

[57] C.A. Johansen and D.F. Mayer, 1990, *Pollinator Protection, A Bee and Pesticide Handbook.*

[58] 2007 NRC study, p. 79.

immune systems all require further study. It seems to us that it is far too early to attempt to link or to dismiss pesticide impacts with CCD.[59]

Even with respect to pesticides known as neonicotinoids (see below), experts disagree about their potential effect on bee health; while some find that dietary neonicotinoids do not appear to be implicated in overall decline of honey bee populations,[60] others attribute unusual bee disappearances and deaths mostly to use of clothianidin (a neonicotinoid) on sunflowers and corn.[61] A 2010 research paper argues that experts and beekeepers may be arguing past each other, changing the definition of the problem depending on the audience. Some French researchers have concluded that at least some French stakeholders have intentionally employed changing definitions deliberately to confuse public understanding.[62]

This section summarizes selected recent studies that have raised questions about the risk to bees posed by chronic exposure to neonicotinoids and certain other pesticides, particularly during the spring planting season.

Generic Pesticide Research

Scientists have tested samples of beebread,[63] trapped pollen,[64] brood nest wax,[65] beeswax foundation,[66] and adult bees and brood and found a broad range of pesticides, including miticides, fungicides, insecticides, and herbicides.[67] Both healthy and unhealthy hives were examined, but no patterns were identified that might point to a particular pesticide or class of pesticides directly affecting bee health.

These same scientists noted that the doses of individual pesticides found in bees were not lethal, but researchers remained concerned about possible chronic problems caused by long-term exposure and possible additive or synergistic effects of exposure to the combinations of pesticides found.[68] Studies have found synergistic adverse effects on honeybees exposed chronically to sublethal concentrations of a pesticide (fipronil or imidacloprid) and *Nosema*.[69]

---

[59] C.A. Mullin, M. Frazier, J.L. Frazier, et al., 2010, "High levels of miticides and agrochemicals in North American apiaries: Implications for honey bee health," *PLoS ONE*, v. 5, n. 3, p. e9754, http://www.plosone.org/article/info%3Adoi%2F10.1371%2Fjournal.pone.0009754.

[60] J. E. Cresswell, N. Desneux, and D. vanEngelsdorp, 2012, "Dietary traces of neonicotinoid pesticides as a cause of population declines in honey bees: an evaluation by Hill's epidemiological criteria," *Pest Management Science*, v. 68, pp. 819-827.

[61] L. Maxim and J.P. van der Sluis, 2010, "Expert explanations of honeybee losses in areas of extensive agriculture in France: Gaucho® compared with other supposed causal factors," *Environmental Research Letters*, v. 5, 014006, http://stacks.iop.org/ERL/5/014006.

[62] Ibid.

[63] Beebread is a pollen mixture stored in honeycomb cells and used with honey by bees as food. Beebread provides nutrition for the queen and brood.

[64] Trapped pollen refers to pollen collected at the entrance to the hive, removed from bees with the use of a trap.

[65] This is wax originating in the area of the hive where brood is reared.

[66] Foundation is the hexagonal sheets of wax and or wax/plastic combination that serves as a basis for comb construction by honey bees.

[67] C.A. Mullin, M. Frazier, J.L. Frazier, et al., 2010, "High levels of miticides and agrochemicals in North American apiaries: Implications for honey bee health," *PLoS ONE*, v. 5, n. 3, p. e9754.

[68] Ibid.

[69] J. Aufauvre, D.G. Biron, C. Vidau, et al. 2012, "Parasite-insecticide interactions: A case study of *Nosema ceranae* (continued...)

Pesticide products include ingredients other than the "active" ingredients which generally receive less scrutiny during registration. Some of these "inerts" are surfactants which are intended to improve delivery of the active ingredient to the target pest. A 2012 study looked at the impact on bee health of three categories of inerts, also known as adjuvants: nonionic surfactants, crop oil concentrates, and organosilicone surfactants.[70] Bee behavior was adversely affected after ingestion of 20 micrograms (µg) of organosilicone surfactant. Nonionic adjuvants also had a small effect, while the crop oil concentrates were inactive, according to the scientists.[71]

Research on Neonicotinoid Pesticides

Neonicotinoids comprise a class of pesticides (that is, active ingredients) that have come under considerable scrutiny with respect to their potential effects on bee health due to an incident of misuse (that is, use not in accord with the pesticide label) of one neonicotinoid, imidacloprid, in Germany[72] that resulted in a large bee kill and widespread beekeeper concerns about use of another neonicotinoid, clothianidin, and its impact on bees in France.[73] Neonicotinoids are systemic pesticides that, regardless of application method (spray, drip irrigation, granular spreading, or seed coating), once taken into the plant migrate into all parts, including flowers, pollen, and nectar.[74] In the United States, some of the most commonly applied neonicotinoids include imidacloprid, clothianidin, and thiamethoxam, which are sold by such tradenames as Admire®, Acceleron®, Axcess®, Attendant®, Belay®, Cruiser®, Gaucho®, Nitro Shield®, Poncho®, and Trimax Pro®. According to scientists at Bayer Crop Science, neonicotinoids accounted for almost 25% of the global pesticide market, and imidacloprid was the largest selling insecticide in the world in 2009.[75]

Exposure to Neonicotinoids

Bees can be exposed to neonicotinoids in many ways. A team of researchers recently reported that they had identified multiple routes of exposure to low levels of neonicotinoids for honey bees living and foraging near agricultural fields planted with corn or soybeans.[76] The highest potential

---

(...continued)

and fipronil synergy on honeybee," *Scientific Reports* 2, 326; C. Vidau, M, Diogon, J. Aufauvre, et al., 2011, "Exposure toe sublethal doses of fipronil and thiacloprid highly increases mortality of honeybees previously infected by *Nosem ceranae*," *PLoS* ONE, v. 6, n. 6, p. e21550; and C. Alaux, J. Brunet, C. Dussaubat, et al., 2012, "Interactions between *Nosema* microspores and a neonicotinoid weaken honeybees (*Apis mellifera*)," *Environmental Microbiology*, v. 12, n. 3. pp. 774-782.

[70] T. J. Ciarlo, C. A. Mullin, James L. Frazier, et al., 2012, "Learning impairment in honey bees caused by agricultural spray adjuvants," *PLoS ONE,* v. 7, n. 7, p. e40848.

[71] Ibid.

[72] D. vanEngelsdorp and M.D. Meixner, 2010, "A historical review of managed honey bee populations in Europe and the United States and factors that may affect them," *Journal of Invertebrate Pathology*, v. 103, Supplement 1, p. S80-S 95.

[73] L. Maxim and J.P. van der Sluis, 2010, "Expert explanations of honeybee losses in areas of extensive agriculture in France: Gaucho® compared with other supposed causal factors," *Environmental Research Letters,* v. 5, http://stacks.iop.org/ERL/5/014006.

[74] UNEP, *Global Honey Bee Colony Disorders and Other Threats to Insect Pollinators*, 2010.

[75] P. Jeschke, R. Nauen, M. Schindler, ,et al., 2011, "Overview of the status and global strategy for neonicotinoids," *Journal of Agricultural and Food Chemistry*, v. 59, pp. 2897-2908.

[76] C. Krupke, G. Hunt, B. Eitzer, et al., 2012, "Multiple routes of pesticide exposure for honey bees living near agricultural fields," *PLoS ONE*, v. 7, n. 1, p. e29268.

---

exposure to the pesticides appeared to occur during planting season, when bee mortality was also high, according to the researchers. Clothianidin was found in about half the corn pollen they sampled, thiamethoxam in three of twenty samples, and fungicides in all pollen samples. Clothianidin was detected in all dead and dying bees but in no healthy bees. Although corn is not an insect-pollinated crop, this research demonstrated that bees forage for corn pollen and take it back to the hive.[77] About half the hive pollen sampled came from corn in this study. In addition, these scientists documented high levels of pesticide in exhaust material from mechanical planters when pesticides and talc were used to coat seeds, and found clothianidin in soil samples from planted and unplanted fields.[78]

Other studies have measured neonicotinoids in pollen and nectar of canola (rape),[79] corn,[80,81] and sunflowers[82,83] grown from seed coated with pesticides. Levels found were below those known to be acutely toxic. However, very recent studies have found that imidacloprid and thiamethoxam concentrations in nectar were greater in squash[84] and pumpkin flowers[85] when insecticide was applied to the soil than they were in canola and sunflowers grown from seed treated with neonicotinoids. Researchers also found metabolites of imidacloprid and thiamethoxam (clothianidin) in all parts of squash plants, along with the parent compound.[86] Krupke et al. found levels of neonicotinoids in bee-collected corn pollen that were similar to levels of imidacloprid determined by other scientists to have sublethal effects potentially affecting colony health.[87] (Some of these studies on the effects of neonicotinoid exposure are described below.)

Another potential source of exposure was suggested by Chengsheng Lu and colleagues, who showed that bees might be exposed to neonicotinoids in the corn syrup they are sometimes fed

---

[77] Ibid.

[78] Ibid.

[79] G. C. Cutler and C. D. Scott-Dupree, 2007, "Exposure to clothianidin seed-treated canola has no long-term impact on honey bees," *Journal of Economic Entomology*, v. 100, pp. 765-772.

[80] J. M. Bonmatin, P. A. Marchand, R. Cahvet, et al., 2005, "Quantification of imidacloprid uptake in maize crops," *Journal of Agricultural and Food Chemistry*, v. 53, pp. 5336-5341.

[81] C. Krupke, G. Hunt, B. Eitzer, et al., 2012, "Multiple routes of pesticide exposure for honey bees living near agricultural fields," *PLoS ONE*, v. 7, n. 1, p. e29268.

[82] F. M. Laurent and E. Rathahao, 2003, "Distribution of [14C] imidacloprid in sunflowers (*Helianthus annuus L.*) following seed treatment," *Journal of Agricultural and Food Chemistry*, v. 51, pp. 8005-8010.

[83] R. Schmuck, R. Schoning, A. Stork, et al., 2001, "Risk posed to honeybees (*Apis mellifera* L, Hymenoptera) by an imidacloprid seed dressing of sunflowers," *Pest Management Science*, v. 57, pp. 225-238.

[84] K. A. Stoner and B. D. Eitzer, 2012, "Movement of soil-applied imidacloprid and thiamethoxam into nectar and pollen of squash (*Cucurbita pepo*)," *PLoS ONE, v. 7, n. 6, p. e39114.*

[85] G. P. Dively and A. Kamel, 2012, "Insecticide residues in pollen and nectar of a cucurbit crop and their potential exposure to pollinators," *Journal of Agricultural and Food Chemistry*, v. 60, pp. 4449-4456.

[86] K. A. Stoner and B. D. Eitzer, 2012, "Movement of soil-applied imidacloprid and thiamethoxam into nectar and pollen of squash (*Cucurbita pepo*)," *PLoS ONE, v. 7, n. 6, p. e39114.*

[87] For example, see H.V.V. Tomé, G.F. Martins, M. August, et al., 2012, "Imidacloprid-induced impairment of mushroom bodies and behavior of the native stingless bee *Melipona quadrifasciata anthidioides*," *PLoS ONE*, v. 7, n. 6, p. e38406; D.M. Eiri and J. C. Nieh, 2012, "A nicotinic cacetylcholine receptor agonist affects honey bee sucrose responsiveness and decreases waggle dancing," *The Journal of Experimental Biology*, v. 215, n. 12, pp. 2022-2029; A. Decourtye, E. Lacassie, and M. Pham-Delegue, 2003, "Learning performances of honey bees (*Apis mellifera L.*) are differentially affected by imidacloprid according to the season." *Pest Management Science*, v. 59, pp. 269-278; or V. Mommaerts, S. Reynders, J. Boulet, et al., 2010, "Risk assessment for side-effects of neonicotinoids against bumblebees with and without impairing foraging behavior," *Ecotoxicology*, v. 19, pp. 207-215.

---

during the winter by beekeepers.[88] However, they did not sample corn syrup actually fed to bees, but rather showed that bees would consume sufficient imidacloprid to produce toxic sublethal effects if they were provided contaminated corn syrup in the hive. Research by DeGrandi-Hoffman, Sammataro, and Simonds found no pesticides in samples of high-fructose corn syrup obtained from three major suppliers.[89]

Effects on Bee Health

Neonicotinoids are insect neurotoxins that vary in strength of effect exerted on honey bees.[90] They are related to nicotine and were developed as an alternative to highly toxic (to humans) organophosphate insecticides such as methyl parathion.[91] Effects on individual bees may be lethal or sublethal depending on dose and other conditions of exposure. For example, EPA has determined that clothianidin "has the potential to be highly toxic on both a contact and an oral basis" to honey bees.[92] In addition, EPA has reported that one honey bee field study submitted to the agency indicates that "mortality, pollen foraging activity, and honey yield were negatively affected by residues of clothianidin," but the residue levels were not reported.[93]

Acute effects also have been demonstrated in another recent field study. It showed that honey bees can be killed by exposure to pesticide-contaminated talc if they fly through dust clouds associated with planting,[94] but mortality appears to depend on high levels of humidity.[95]

In response to reports that honey bees are disappearing and causing hives to collapse, recent studies of the impacts of exposure to imidacloprid and other neonicotinoids[96,97] have focused more on their potential to affect complex behaviors in insects, including flight, navigation, olfactory memory, recruitment, foraging, and coordination.[98] One study has reported sublethal

---

[88] Chensheng Lu, K.M. Warchol, and R.A. Callahan, 2012, "In situ replication of honey bee colony collapse disorder," *Bulletin of Insectology*, v. 65, n. 1 99-106.

[89] G. DeGrandi-Hoffman, D. Sammataro, and R. Simonds, 2012, "Are agrochemicals present in high fructose corn syrup fed to honey bees (*Apis mellifera* L.)?" *Jurnal of Apicultural Research*, v. 51, n. 4, pp. 371-372.

[90] D. Laurino, M. Porporato, A. Patetta, et al., 2011, "Toxicity of neonicotinoid insecticides to honey bees: laboratory tests," *Bulletin of Insectology*, v. 64, n. 1, pp. 107-113.

[91] S. P. Bradbury, Office of Pesticide Programs, Letter to Peter T. Jenkins, Center for Food Safety and International Center for Technology Assessment, July 17, 2012. Hereafter referred to as Bradbury response to citizen petition.

[92] J. DeCant and M. Barrett, 2010, "Environmental Fate and Ecological Risk Assessment for the Registration of CLOTHIANIDIN for Use as a Seed Treatment on Mustard Seed (Oilseed and Condiment) and Cotton," EPA/Office of Prevention, Pesticides and Toxic Substances, Office of Pesticide Programs, Washington, DC, p. 14.

[93] Ibid.

[94] A. Tapparo, D. Marton, C. Giorio, et al., 2012, "Assessment of the environmental exposure of honeybees to particulate matter containing neonicotinoid insecticides coming from corn coated seeds," *Environmental Science & Technology*, v.46, pp. 2592-2599.

[95] V. Girolami, M. Marzaro, L. Vivian, et al., 2012, "Fatal powdering of bees in flight with particulates of neonicotinoids seed coating and humidity implication," *Journal of Applied Entomology*, v. 136, n. 1-2, pp. 17-26.

[96] D. Cox-Foster and D. vanEngelsdorp, "Solving the Mystery of the Vanishing Bees," *Scientific American*, March 31, 2009; Northwest Coalition for Alternatives to Pesticides, "Imidacloprid, Fact Sheet," *Journal of Pesticide Reform*, Spring 2001, http://www.pesticide.org/imidacloprid.pdf; and Apiculteurs de France, "Composite Document of Present Position Relating to Gaucho, Sunflower and Bees," http://www.beekeeping.com/articles/us/gaucho/manifestation_paris_us.htm.

[97] Joe Cummins, "Neoniccotinoid insecticides used in seed dressing may be responsible for the collapse of honeybee colonies," April 24, 2007, http://www.organicconsumers.org/articles/article_4972.cfm.

[98] BNA's *International Environmental Law Committee Newsletter*, vol. 11, no. 1, February 2009, (continued...)

---

effects of neonicotinoid pesticides on honey bee foraging behavior that may impair the navigational and foraging abilities of honey bees.[99] Scientists at Bayer Crop Science argue that the dose of thiamethoxam delivered to bees in this case was not "field-relevant."[100] At "field-relevant" doses for sunflowers and canola (defined as 0.15 nanogram (ng) per bee of imidacloprid or 0.05 ng/bee of clothianidin), Schneider et al. found no effect on foraging and homing behavior of honey bees exposed to treated crops.[101] The same study found, that "both substances led to a significant reduction of foraging activity and to longer foraging flights at doses of 1.5 ng/bee of imidacloprid or 0.5 ng/bee of clothianidin during the first three hours after treatment."[102] However, these latter numbers might be approaching "field relevant" numbers for neonicotinoids in squash nectar and corn pollen (see discussion of exposure above), particularly when other sources of exposure are considered and when pesticides are applied directly to soil.[103]

Other studies have found impaired brood development[104] and increased rates of *Nosema* infection in honey bees exposed to sublethal pesticide levels.[105] Imidacloprid ingestion by stingless bee larvae at rates above 0.0056 µg/bee decreased survival rates, negatively affected development of a specific region of the bee brain called the mushroom body, and impaired walking behavior of newly emerged adult worker bees.[106] Scientists from Bayer Crop Science have criticized one of the studies linking neonicotinoid exposure with *Nosema* infection because it was conducted in the laboratory and not under field conditions.[107]

In another study, responsiveness to sucrose and waggle dancing (which communicates food locations to nest mates) was adversely affected when honey bees ingested a few nanograms of imidacloprid. The bees' preference for greater sucrose concentrations dissipated within an hour of ingestion.[108]

(...continued)

http://www.abanet.org/environ/committees/intenviron/newsletter/feb09/IELC_Feb09.pdf.

[99] M. Henry, M. Beguin, F. Requier, et al., 2012, "A common pesticide decreases foraging success and survival in honey bees," *Science*, v. 336, n. 6079, pp. 348-350.

[100] Bayer Crop Science, "Overview of recent publications on neonicotinoids and pollinators." Paper received personally from Jean Reimers (CropLife America), June 20, 2012.

[101] C.W. Schneider, J. Tautz, B. Grünewald, et al., 2012, "RFID Tracking of sublethal effects of two neonicotinoid insecticides on the foraging behavior of *Apis mellifera*." PLoS ONE, v. 7, n. 1, p. e30023, http://www.plosone.org/article/info%3Adoi%2F10.1371%2Fjournal.pone.0030023.

[102] Ibid.

[103] K. A. Stoner and B. D. Eitzer, 2012, "Movement of soil-applied imidacloprid and thiamethoxam into nectar and pollen of squash (*Cucurbita pepo*)," *PLoS ONE, v. 7, n. 6, p. e39114*.

[104] Judy Y. Wu, Carol M. Anelli, and Walter S. Sheppard, 2011, "Sub-lethal effects of pesticide residues in brood comb on worker honey bee (*Apis mellifera*) development and longevity," *PLoS ONE* v., 6, n. 2, p. e14720.

[105] J.Y. Wu, M.D. Smart, C.M. Anelli, et al., 2012, "Honey bees (*Apis mellifera*) reared in brood combs containing high levels of pesticide residues exhibit increased susceptibility to *Nosema* (Microsporidia) infection," *Journal of Invertebrate Pathology*, v. 109, pp. 326-329; and J. Pettis, D. vanEngelsdorp, J. Johnson, et al., 2012, "Pesticide exposure in honey bees results in increased levels of the gut pathogen *Nosema*," *Naturwissenschaften*, v. 99, pp. 153-158.

[106] H. V. V. Tomé, G. F. Martins, M. August, et al., 2012, "Imidacloprid-induced impairment of mushroom bodies and behavior of the native stingless bee Melipona quadrifasciata anthidioides," PLoS ONE, v. 7, n. 6, p. e38406.

[107] Bayer Crop Science, "Overview of recent publications on neonicotinoids and pollinators." Paper received personally from Jean Reimers (CropLife America), June 20, 2012.

[108] D. M. Eiri and J. C. Nieh, 2012, "A nicotinic cacetylcholine receptor agonist affects honey bee sucrose responsiveness and decreases waggle dancing," *The Journal of Experimental Biology*, v. 215, n. 12, pp. 2022-2029.

Finally, in another recent experiment, 16 hives of honey bees were fed corn syrup treated with imidacloprid. After 6 months, 15 of the 16 treated hives collapsed, while 4 untreated control hives remained healthy.[109]

A few recent studies have looked at bumble bees. One found that bumble bee colonies exposed in a laboratory to low levels of imidacloprid had a significantly reduced growth rate and an 85% reduction in queen production relative to untreated colonies.[110] Another study found that ingestion of low concentrations of neonicotinoids could adversely affect foraging behavior.[111] Bayer Crop Science argues that these results were obtained "under artificial conditions and are in conflict with" earlier studies.[112]

Neonicotinoid Registration Review at EPA

Neonicotinoid pesticide registrations currently are being reviewed by EPA. EPA's website states:

> The neonicotinoids are a class of insecticides with a common mode of action that affects the central nervous system of insects, causing paralysis and death. All of the neonicotinoids were registered after 1984 and were not subject to reregistration. Some uncertainties have been identified since their initial registration regarding the potential environmental fate and effects of neonicotinoid pesticides, particularly as they relate to pollinators. Data suggest that neonicotinic residues can accumulate in pollen and nectar of treated plants and may represent a potential exposure to pollinators. Adverse effects data as well as beekill incidents have also been reported, highlighting the potential direct and/or indirect effects of neonicotinic pesticides. Therefore, among other refinements to ecological risk assessment during registration review, the Agency will consider potential effects of the neonicotinoids to honeybees and other pollinating insects.[113]

Review of clothianidin registrations began December 2011. EPA aims to review all neonicotinoids as a group.[114]

In the process of reviewing registrations for neonicotinoids, EPA is revising its risk assessment process. A letter from the Environmental Fate and Effects Division of the EPA Office of Chemical Safety and Pollution Prevention explains:

> The EPA is currently revising its process for assessing pesticide risks to bees to reflect advancements in the state of the science that underlie bee exposure and effects assessments. Interim guidance [EPA, 2011, Pesticides: Science and Policy, Interim Guidance on Honey Bee

---

[109] Chensheng Lu, K.M. Warchol, and R.A. Callahan, 2012, "In situ replication of honey bee colony collapse disorder," *Bulletin of Insectology*, v. 65, n. 1 99-106.

[110] P.R. Whitehorn, S. O'Connor, D. Goulson, et al. 2012, "Neonicotinoid pesticide reduces bumble bee colony growth and queen production," *Science*, v. 336, p. 351-352.

[111] V. Mommaerts, S. Reynders, J. Boulet, et al., 2010, "Risk assessment for side-effects of neonicotinoids against bumblebees with and without impairing foraging behavior," *Ecotoxicology*, v. 19, pp. 207-215.

[112] Bayer Crop Science, "Overview of recent publications on neonicotinoids and pollinators." Paper received personally from Jean Reimers (CropLife America), June 20, 2012.

[113] EPA, Pesticides, Registration Review, Program Highlights, Groups of Related Pesticides Beginning Registration Review, Neonicotinoids, May 9, 2012, http://www.epa.gov/oppsrrd1/registration_review/highlights.htm, Dec. 4, 2012.

[114] The status of the review and relevant documents is available at http://www.regulations.gov (docket: EPA-HQ-OPP-2011-0865). EPA review of imidacloprid registrations began December 2008 (docket: EPA-HQ-OPP-2008-0844). The schedule for other reviews is at http://www.epa.gov/oppfead1/cb/ppdc/2012/may/session-9-reg-review-update.pdf.

Data Requirements, http://www.epa.gov/pesticides/science/efed/policy_guidance/team_authors/ terrestrial_biology_tech_team/honeybee_data_interim_guidance.pdf] on factors to consider when evaluating exposure and effects to bees is available to ecological risk assessors. In 2012, the EPA will present to a FIFRA Scientific Advisory Panel (SAP) a proposed process for quantifying risks to honeybees and identifying exposure and effect studies needed to inform that process. Based on input from the SAP, the EPA will incorporate its revised assessment process to quantify risks to bees in a similar manner as that used to evaluate risks to other taxa.[115]

The draft risk assessment policy has been released to the public, and the materials distributed and discussed at the SAP meeting are available in the regulatory docket (EPA-HQ-OPP-2012-0543).

On March 20, 2012, EPA received a citizen petition asking it to suspend registrations for the insecticide clothianidin, among other demands.[116] The petition and numerous supplemental submissions of research reports and opinions are posted in the regulatory docket on the Internet at http://www.regulations.gov. EPA responded in part to the petition on July 17, 2012. EPA denied the request to suspend registrations "to prevent imminent harm" because the petitioners did not meet the burden of proof for registration suspension. However, EPA plans to revisit this decision and to evaluate the other demands in the near future as it reviews neonicotinoid registrations.

Author Contact Information

Linda-Jo Schierow
Specialist in Environmental Policy
lschierow@crs.loc.gov, 7-7279

Renée Johnson
Specialist in Agricultural Policy
rjohnson@crs.loc.gov, 7-9588

M. Lynne Corn
Specialist in Natural Resources Policy
lcorn@crs.loc.gov, 7-7267

---

[115] EPA, Environmental Fate and Effects Division (EFED), EFED Response to Comments Submitted to the Clothianidin Registration Review Docket (Docket ID: EPA-HQ-OPP-2011-0865), June 11, 2012, p. 3.

[116] S.P. Bradbury, EPA Office of Pesticide Programs, Letter to Peter T. Jenkins, Center for Food Safety and International Center for Technology Assessment, "Clothianidin Emergency Citizen Petition dated March 20, 2012," July 17, 2012, http://www.epa.gov/opp00001/about/intheworks/epa-respns-to-clothianidin-petition-17july12.pdf.